Trout

A Buddy Book by
Deborah Coldiron

ABDO
Publishing Company

UNDERWATER
WORLD

VISIT US AT
www.abdopublishing.com

Published by ABDO Publishing Company, 8000 West 78th Street, Edina, Minnesota 55439.

Copyright © 2009 by Abdo Consulting Group, Inc. International copyrights reserved in all countries. No part of this book may be reproduced in any form without written permission from the publisher. Buddy Books™ is a trademark and logo of ABDO Publishing Company.

Printed in the United States.

Coordinating Series Editor: Sarah Tieck
Contributing Editor: Michael P. Goecke
Graphic Design: Deborah Coldiron
Cover Photograph: Photos.com
Interior Photographs/Illustrations: Brandon Cole Marine Photography (pages 15, 17, 20, 21); Clipart.com (page 13); iStockphoto.com: Scott Leigh (page 28); Minden Pictures: Michael Durham (page 19), Tim Fitzharris (page 19), Frans Lanting (page 21), Michael Quinton (page 9); Photos.com (pages 5, 11, 21, 23, 24, 25, 27); SeaPics.com: Pat Clayton (page 9); U.S. Fish & Wildlife Service: Eric Engbretson (pages 9, 21, 22), Lloyde Hazzard (page 30), Greg A. Syverson (page 7)

Library of Congress Cataloging-in-Publication Data

Coldiron, Deborah.
  Trout / Deborah Coldiron.
     p. cm. -- (Underwater world)
  Includes index.
  ISBN 978-1-60453-139-8
  1. Trout--Juvenile literature. 2. Trout--Juvenile literatura. I. Title.

QL638.S2C63 2009
597.5'7--dc22
                                                            2008005053

Table Of Contents

The World Of Trout

Every living creature needs water. Some animals not only need water, they live in it, too.

Scientists have found more than 250,000 kinds of plants and animals living underwater. And, they believe there could be one million more! The trout is one animal that makes its home in this underwater world.

Water covers 70 percent of Earth's surface.

The trout is a fast fish with strong teeth. Dark spots and tiny scales cover its skin. There is a small, fatty fin near its tail. This is called an adipose fin.

Trout mainly live in cool, freshwater rivers or streams. But, some trout live in lakes or oceans.

Both salmon and some trout migrate between freshwater rivers and saltwater oceans.

There is great variety among trout. So, it is hard for scientists to say how many **species** exist. But in North America, there are about ten known species.

Rainbow trout *(top)*, cutthroat trout *(center)*, and golden trout *(bottom)* are North American trout species.

A Closer Look

Trout have **streamlined** bodies that were made to move! Also, they are **aggressive** hunters. This combination makes them very popular with fishermen.

Some fishermen use a method called fly-fishing to catch trout in shallow streams. They attach special lightweight bait to their lines. The bait moves like insects on the water's surface. This draws in trout.

River and stream trout are much smaller than lake and ocean trout. Adult river and stream trout may weigh just one pound (.5 kg). Ocean and lake trout may weigh 100 pounds (45 kg)!

The Body Of A Trout

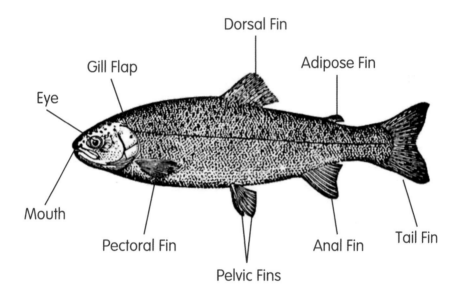

Dorsal Fin

Adipose Fin

Gill Flap

Eye

Mouth

Pectoral Fin

Pelvic Fins

Anal Fin

Tail Fin

A Growing Trout

Adult trout gather in freshwater streams to **spawn** between spring and autumn. Some of them have been living in the ocean. These trout may travel great distances to reproduce in their home streams.

A female trout finds an area of loose gravel on the streambed. There, she digs a hole in the rocks. This serves as a nest.

FAST FACTS

Loose gravel is good for trout egg nests. It allows water to flow freely around the eggs. This supplies oxygen to the eggs.

A trout's nest is known as a redd.
A female trout may dig and fill
many redds while spawning.

A male trout **fertilizes** the eggs after the female lays them. After two or three months, the eggs hatch. These tiny trout are called fry.

When fry grow strong enough, they leave the nest. Then, they are called fingerlings. Fingerlings eat **plankton**.

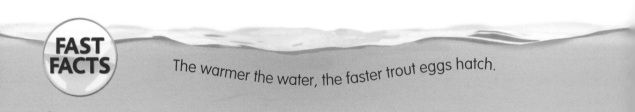

The warmer the water, the faster trout eggs hatch.

Female trout cover fertilized eggs with gravel to protect them. But, they do not stay and guard their redds. Newly hatched trout are on their own!

Most trout spend their entire lives in freshwater. But, some leave for the ocean after one or two years.

A Mystery

Rainbow trout and steelhead trout are the same **species**. But, they live very different lives. Rainbow trout live in freshwater. Steelhead trout **migrate** to large lakes or the ocean.

Rainbow trout are much smaller than steelhead trout. They may grow to 18 inches (46 cm) in length. Steelhead trout may be more than 30 inches (76 cm) long!

It is unusual for one fish species to live in such different ways. Scientists are studying how and why these trout do this.

Rainbow trout often have colorful patterns on their sides.

Steelhead trout are steely blue. Their jaws become hook shaped as they grow.

Family Connections

Trout belong to the family Salmonidae. This group of fish also includes salmon and char.

All salmonid have fins made of thin skin stretched over fine spines. Trout and salmon also have adipose fins.

Like trout, salmon are born in freshwater. They migrate to the ocean to feed and grow. Later, they return to freshwater to reproduce. After spawning season, most salmon die.

A male salmon changes as it moves between salt water *(top left)* and freshwater *(top right)* to breed. Its jaws curve inward, forming a hook. A hump grows on its back. And, its body may turn a bright red orange color.

Lake trout *(top left)* and brook trout *(top right)* are often mistaken for trout. But they are char! Char have pale spots, while trout have dark ones.

Dinnertime

Trout eat flies, crickets, and many other insects. They also eat fish eggs, small fish, and small **crustaceans** (kruhs-TAY-shuhns). Very young trout feed mostly on **plankton**.

Crayfish are small freshwater crustaceans that become tasty trout meals.

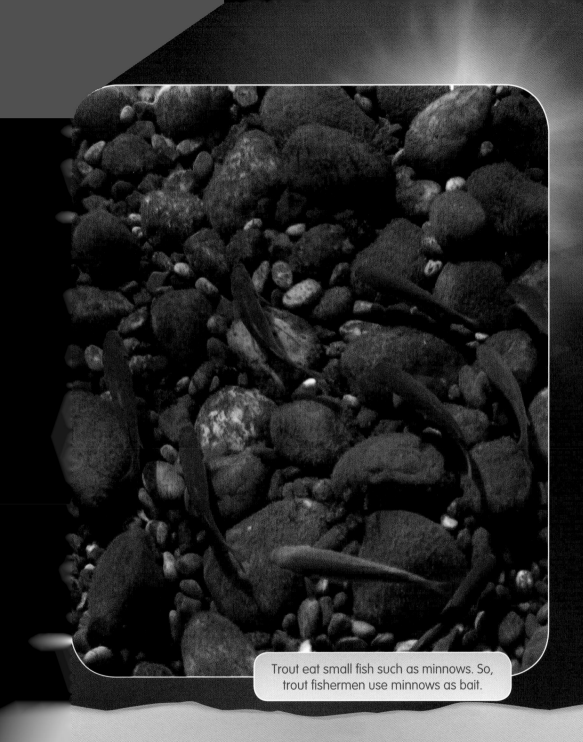

Trout eat small fish such as minnows. So, trout fishermen use minnows as bait.

A World Of Danger

The biggest dangers to trout come from humans. Overfishing, water pollution, and loss of natural **habitat** are among the worst dangers.

Otters are also a danger to trout. But, they are a natural predator.

Special ladders help migrating fish swim over dams.

Dams can block movement for many kinds of fish, including trout.

Dams challenge trout **migrating** in rivers and streams. And, logging practices can harm trout streams.

Global warming is also a danger to trout. Even a small temperature increase could make many streams unlivable for trout.

FAST FACTS

Trout require cool water to survive. They prefer water that is 50 to 60 degrees Fahrenheit (10 to 16°C). Many trout streams are already close to the high end of this range.

Many trout streams are shallow and fast moving.

Fascinating Facts

🐟 Sport fishermen use a method called trolling to catch large lake and ocean trout. They trail baited lines from moving boats.

Trolling

Trout are native to Earth's Northern **Hemisphere**. But, humans have **introduced** rainbow trout in more than 40 countries. They now live in rivers and streams on every continent except Antarctica!

Some introduced trout have harmed their new homes. In South America and Australia, trout have eaten large numbers of native fish. They also compete for available food and spread disease.

Learn And Explore

Trout are often raised in hatcheries. These special fish farms supply rivers, streams, and lakes with extra fish.

Another way many U.S. states protect trout populations is by charging the fishermen fees. The money raised goes to protect and restock trout in heavily fished areas.

Some hatcheries clip off a trout's adipose fin before releasing it into the wild. This helps identify farm-raised fish.

IMPORTANT WORDS

aggressive displaying hostility.

crustacean any of a group of animals with hard shells that live mostly in water. Crabs, lobsters, and shrimp are all crustaceans.

fertilize to make fertile. Something that is fertile is capable of growing or developing.

global warming an increase in the average temperature of Earth's surface.

habitat a place where a living thing is naturally found.

hemisphere one half of Earth.

introduce to bring in, especially for the first time.

migrate to move from one place to another, often to find food.

plankton small animals and plants that float in a body of water.

spawn to produce eggs.

species living things that are very much alike.

streamlined having a shape that reduces the resistance to motion when moving through air or water.

WEB SITES

To learn more about trout, visit ABDO Publishing Company on the World Wide Web. Web sites about trout are featured on our Book Links page. These links are routinely monitored and updated to provide the most current information available.

www.abdopublishing.com

INDEX